In memory of my brother Donald
who is now able to answer some of my troubling questions

Contents

Tributes and End Time

Childhood Memories

Nature and Others

Foreword

I am so pleased that Emerson Wiens has collected these poems he titles *Coming to Terms.* Those of us who come to creative writing late perhaps lose out on the record of our youthful anger and idealism, and our poems perhaps go without some measure of the romance and awe of youthful writers, but we are blessed with the worldly wisdom we have accumulated, an eye for historical detail, conscious of a longer view of time, have perhaps attained some serenity about what life will give and take, and in Emerson's case, evidence an amazing tolerance and fair-mindedness with a heaping tablespoon of grace remembering the details of a life.

I well remember when he first came to my class to write poems. A longtime academician who leaned toward the philosophical, Emerson was bursting with enthusiasm for writing this form, which made room for the details of one's existence, the personal, the remembered. I loved his vulnerability, his willingness to write what he knew, not much corralled by his long academic career—though he had long been known for his plainspokenness, honesty and integrity on the Bethel College campus. When he played in poetry and with words, he was artful, as perhaps he knew how to be with what were once known as "industrial and technological arts." He seemed to have experienced a certain liberation in this "telling in words," and he was curious to see what he would find. And just as he polished wood in the art forms that he sculpted, with just such a keen eye, he loved rewriting, rethinking, polishing, playing and rearranging on the page. It is so good now to see what his roving mind has uncovered over the years.

At the center of Emerson's work is his keen eye for whimsical observation and his keen ear, which hears another's voice and heart. Using those, he does indeed, as his title poem suggests, "come to terms" as one does in choosing words to observe, but not really! For

Emerson, the prober, will not really ever come to terms as long as he is poking his pen under rocks to see what is really going on. So, "coming to terms" is a guise for ranging philosophically and tenderly over many hard topics—aging, heritage, dreams, values, a career, relationships—but Emerson will always say a valiant NO! to lack of tolerance, bigotry, and hypocrisy. And he will always say YES! to whimsy, the look askance, the raised eyebrow of surprise, the chance meeting. Maybe it is my own awareness of the years moving on, but Emerson's valiant, honest look at death in some of these poems moved me most!

I find in this collection of poems some trademark traits of the voice and spirit of Emerson's poems. Religious questions will always rile this poet's sometimes guilt-stricken voice. Unjust policies might make it strident. "What If?" questions will always lure this poet's eye. The beauty of the human spirit in its diverse intercultural and international manifestations will always offer a route to acceptance: "No need for a nervous breakdown." Watching the years pass will mellow him: "Only the fluent mockingbird atop the deserted house" can really tell! Fishing will tame him. Gratitude will haunt him. Patience and the wry smile will stalk his inquiries as long as he lives.

Raylene Hinz-Penner, Lecturer, Washburn University, March 2012

Dialogue

You ask, How do you write?
In a quiet place, I say:
the coffee shop, my favorite.
Writers come here for a purpose~
not to be entertained,
to discuss the nature of the universe,
or the changing weather.
People pass, speaking in muffled tones,
recognizing the sacredness of this place,
a place where expression is born.
The espresso cup bangs to release
its contents; cream? Again silence.
The pen touches the paper, waiting.
The first line begins the dialogue . . .

The Human Condition

Coming to Terms

I'm coming to terms ~
    with failing body parts:
    thinning cartilage, leaky valves,
    sleep apnea, enlarged prostate; reluctant muscles~
    used to grab the rim, now can't touch the net,
    with a body owned by medical specialists.

I'm coming to terms ~
    with the results of activities when I was young
    and invincible: football-induced seizures,
    hernias, stomach ulcers, pre-cancerous
    skin lesions, clogged arteries.
    progressive hearing loss.

I'm coming to terms ~
    with a mouth more synthetic than natural:
    bridges, crowns, porcelain, gold;
    with eyeglasses large enough
    to contain the whole prescription,
    with print too small to read.

I'm coming to terms ~
    with retirement: no more office,
    no halls of ivy; no more lectures,
    thesis committees, papers to grade;
    no annual reports or peer-reviewed articles to write;
    no adrenaline rush, accolades, no tenure track.

I'm coming to terms ~
    with my ancestors:
    their courage, strength, and wisdom;
    their sacrifices and hardships.
    Honoring their commitments, their values
    that have influenced my actions, my path.

I'm coming to terms ~
    with aging relationships,
    deceased parents and friends before their time;
    with intimacy strained by distance, disease, dementia;
    with friendships modified by
    decades of separate paths.

I'm coming to terms ~
    with dreams unfulfilled:
    travels not taken, sights not seen,
    manuscripts not written.
    with gratitude unexpressed,
    friendships not nurtured.

I'm coming to terms ~
    with my failings;
    when I betrayed the trust someone had in me;
    when I spoke in anger and damaged a relationship;
    when I wasn't the husband and father I should have been;
    when I failed to be a model of love and compassion.

I'm coming to terms ~
    with my tendency to let work dominate my life
    at the expense of relationships;
    with my lack of patience, flexibility, and acceptance;
    with my failure to appreciate adequately the gift of life
    and the beauty that surrounds me.

I'm coming to terms ~
    with the realization that I will not make a great
    contribution to society; no Henry Ford or Robert Frost;
    with the fact that I am ordinary; my acts, my life
    will soon be forgotten like the lives
    of most who have gone before me.

I'm coming to terms –
    with my departure from this life.
    After my physical presence is gone,
    nothing will remain but reflections
    of who I was, what I did, until the
    gusts of time blur the images.

I'm coming to terms ~
    with a life richly blessed: parents who believed in me;
    teachers and friends who stretched me;
    three children who challenged me to
    think beyond my limited world view;
    a wife of 56 years who loves me despite my idiosyncrasies.

I'm coming to terms ~
    with my faith: what is true, what is myth, whether it matters.
    With questions about God: is God an energy force, a process,
    an action, a super human, a culturally defined entity?
    None of the above? With the knowledge
    that I will never know for sure in this lifetime.

I still have **not** come to terms ~
    with those who are prejudiced, intolerant, and bigoted,
    with those who start wars and make God in their own image,
    with those who rape the environment in the name of progress;
    with those who consider consumption and accumulation
    the highest measures of human accomplishment.

But, I am still coming to terms ~
    with my limitations~an aging body, slower mind.
    But life is still fresh, exciting, vibrant!
    Music still thrills me; friends and family stimulate
    and challenge. The world of ideas that has marked
    my journey still draws me into its web.

I'm coming to terms ~
    with my waning years.
    My search for truth and meaning, my attempts
    to integrate faith and reason, are still compelling.
    Like the Apostle Paul, I see through a glass darkly,
    yet discipleship can still be a clear choice.

I will continue to encourage respect and
    affection for the natural world.
    I will strive in my own small way to shape a world
    in which justice, equality, and love prevail.
    I pray that I be given the grace and clarity of mind
    to live my remaining years to their fullest.

Morning Edition

(Courtesy, KHCC, Wichita, KS)

The Israeli Chief of Staff has warned the troops
not to use force you knocked the alarm clock
off the headboard again the students from the only
college for the deaf are in the third day
of protesting the appointment of a president who
is not hearing if you heard what I said
why didn't you answer me up the coast at Fort Charles
a totally different atmosphere exists the Royals
have moved their spring training to a 13 million
dollar lunch money or do you want to take
a packed lunch today Kansas has many laws but
is weak on enforcement now what do you want
for breakfast according to the poll
the evangelicals and born-again Christians
crossed over toast and oatmeal his Contra
aid proposal was voted down and his
attorney general continues to be under
fire for destroying evidence clean the water
spots off the mirror please George Bush
wiped out Dole's lead with his consistent
wins in the South why don't you roll the toilet
paper back up when you're northerly winds
10 to 15 miles per hour with little to no
precipitation it's 7:45 time to go at
the Olympics the Soviets have now won 26
medals do you want horseradish on your sand she
has gained a reputation in her poetry for writing
about the struggles of young since you
died without warning Mom turn off the radio.

The Gift

Tom and Mary Jane had a baby,
a bouncing, boisterous baby boy.
They thanked God for this beautiful gift.
Daniel grew fast, learned quickly, always
happy; a real joy to his parents.

On his fourth birthday, Mary Jane
suspicioned anemia. She was wrong.
"Leukemia," said the doctor.
"Can't be!" parents unisoned.
"Not this, our precious gift from God!"

Treatment was painful;
the golden curls vanished.
But the smile somehow remained.
He did not know that he would not
join his friends in kindergarten.

"God, where are you?" his parents asked.
"Jesus said, 'Ask and you shall receive.'
Was that some kind of joke?"
Tom and Mary Jane pleaded,
begged, cried out to God. No response.

The agony, the searching for answers
did not stop after Daniel's body was laid
in the little coffin. "Where are you, God?
How could you do this to Daniel,
his whole life ahead of him?

"How could you do this to us,
your faithful followers?
Surely he would have been a follower.
Were the scriptures wrong?
Was Jesus deceived,

"Or was the promise conditional,
dependent on something, but what?
What is more precious than life?
Is not life the greatest gift
You have given us?

"Why would You take it away
from an innocent child?
Are you not a personal God?
Do You not number the hairs on my head?
Do You not know when the sparrow falls?

"Is this why Jesus said, 'My God, my God,
why have You forsaken me?'
Were You never there from the start?"

Redbird in the Window

Redbird, redbird,
Why do you claw the cardinal in the window?
Do you not recognize the image as your own?
Whom are you attacking? What is it that you fear?
Defending yourself from a competitor?

Protecting the nest hidden in the sumac,
containing fertile eggs, awaiting wings?
Where is that song that brought
joy to the neighborhood?

Redbird, redbird, time has passed.
The nest vacant, the sumac bare;
green leaves lost to frost and wind.
Only shell fragments and snow crystals now.

Why do you still attack the intruder in the window?
From whence comes your paranoia?
He has never harmed you; never escaped his glass prison.
Yet day after day you charge the menacing image.

Am I not the redbird, beating my wings
against the glass, claws extended,
obsessed by fears that dominate my thoughts?
Fears of rejection, failure, insecurity, illness?

Where is that song of my youth, of hope and joy
that once made others smile? Now, only
a melody of desperation, fear, and foreboding
that leaves me isolated, alone, depressed.

But I am not the redbird!
The image in the glass is only a mirage.
Fears are not reality.
Why do I allow them to control me?

I must focus on the beauty that surrounds me,
not on the internal fears that threaten to paralyze.
I must experience the God of hope,
joy, and peace within me, within all of us.

Sunday Worship

We come to worship Sunday morning,
drawn by a common heritage,
convenience of location,
desire for social interaction,
or need to church the children.

Stained glass windows bathe the sanctuary
in rainbow light. The organ prelude, so calming,
so soothing! The children's story, so entertaining!
The choir, so talented and professional!
So inspirational! What was it they sang?

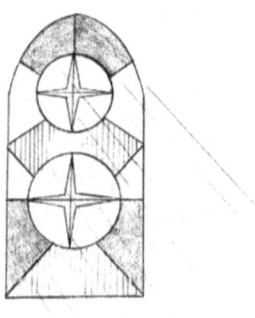

We hear the same words, same music,
an experience modified by personal expectations.
We come to worship, a little; come to
be challenged, but not much. For a moment,
God, help us to forget the ills of the world.

We want to hear about those in need, a little.
About our missionary program, but not much.
About our budget needs, but my money is committed.
About those who have died or are hospitalized.
Sorry, but have no time to visit.

The preacher is so eloquent, so scholarly;
her stories so interesting and illustrative.
But, what were the three points?
What? We are responsible for people in need
and God's creation? Is that in the by-laws?

My lifestyle is sacred! It will not
be compromised! Who does God think He/She is?
So pleasant to relax here in the pew
away from my exciting, egocentric life.
I'll make my grocery list during the offertory.

I am renewed, ready to face another hectic week.
What would we do without Sunday worship?

Questions

Once secure and content with tradition,
my parents' religion sufficient for me;
no questions, no doubts, contradictions ignored.
But the religion was not mine~

like borrowed furniture, rental property;
drinking from a used cup.
How do I make it mine?
Or is there nothing to own?

Some say God is everywhere, in everything.
Are you in the scampering cockroach,
the loaf of bread, the mold on my cheese?
Or are you restricted to human presence?

Where are you, God? Are you the God of nature?
In the destructive power of the hurricane?
In my next door neighbor, whoever he/she is?
Or embedded in my psyche?

The biologist proclaims, "God is process~evolution."
A theologian says, "God is creativity."
How does one worship creativity or evolution,
or is worship an empty, obsolete response?

Is theology itself archaic, irrelevant?
The sociologist says America has many gods:
the god that accepts gays, and the god that rejects,
the god that condemns abortion, the god that accepts,

the god of the Republican party,
the god of the Democrats.
The rabbi says right practice is
more important than right theology.

So is God a noun that
identifies? A verb that acts?
An adjective that describes, or a process, i.e.,
that constant in the universe that explains?

Or, are God and religion only human constructs~
ways to explain what we do not understand?
A means to provide ultimate justice
for those who were evil on earth?

Is the concept of life after death
a human fabrication because humans cannot face
extinction? Do we forget that we had no history
before we became a fertilized egg?

The scriptures say where two or three
are gathered in your name, you are there.
But how can we gather in your name
if we don't know your name?

Does God not exist if we are alone~
overlooking the grandeur of the canyon?
considering the intricate beauty of DNA?
holding our firstborn for the first time?

The Old Testament describes God as
a God of anger and judgment, who is
territorial and exclusive. Or was this
only man's misguided understanding?

The New Testament shows an inclusive God.
Rollins states that God is bigger, better,
yet different than our understanding of God.[1]
If God is mystery, beyond my understanding,

how do I avoid the idolatry of imagining God,
or the relativism of pure reason?
How can one experience a God of otherness,
unknowable by human intellect?

Must all my questions be answered for me
to live? The book says God is love. Jesus
showed us that love is a verb. Can one accept
Jesus' teachings while rejecting all images of God?

---

1   Peter Rollins, *How (not) to Speak of God*, page 19.

Pictures on the Bedroom Wall

#1, #2

My grandparents, immigrants from
southern Russia where their ancestors
had fled to avoid religious persecution
a century earlier. But Catherine
the Great no longer present.

#3

My father, trumpet in hand, member
of a local band; couldn't afford lessons.
Later took up the violin.
What determination, he
with a sixth grade education!

#4

My mother in a white dress,
sitting, hands folded;
graduation from the academy.
A sly smile hinting of a sense
of humor that would later enrich my life.

#5

Their wedding picture dated 1923.
Father sitting erect, dark, three-piece
suit, white shirt, light tie
white boutonniere. Mother,
cradling a simple bouquet,

standing beside him,
hand on his shoulder.
White dress, no train, short veil.
My father in his thirties,
eight years her senior.

What were their dreams?
A farm of their own?
A large family to help
with field work and chores?
Travels to see the world?

#6
The 25th anniversary pose;
family now complete.
Three sons, two daughters
Mother's soft smile masking
her crippling arthritis.

The dream farm in Colorado
lost in the Great Depression,
the extended drought–the Dust Bowl.
Returned to Kansas penniless,
began again on a tenant farm.

Un-insulated house with dust
drifts on the windowsills.
No running water, no electricity.
Implements used or borrowed.
But unflagging determination and faith.

#7
Golden wedding pose:
Mother's face more creased;
Father's hair silver white. Retired
comfortably in town, their own cottage:
indoor plumbing, electricity, insulation.

Their children all established:
Kansas to Japan, Denver to Illinois.
Twelve grandchildren, scattered.
But Mother, with a weak heart,
will not finish the decade.

What have their struggles taught us,
their children? What values and faith
were instilled in our formative years?
What principles for living did
they model? How much we owe!

The next picture, mine.
What will my children say?
What story will they tell?
What values have I taught?

Journey Out of Darkness

My days have turned dark and threatening.
Fear has replaced joy and happiness.
Why? I ask. Why has life become devastating?
I turn to God: Why me? Why now?
Help me through this darkness,

this blinding forest of night.
Give me back the joy of living.
God does not respond, does not explain.
My fears are unbearable.
My self-confidence shredded.

"Classic depression," the therapist is confident.
Is it better or worse than contemporary
depression? I immerse myself in my studies.
I avoid people; crowds terrify me!
Panic attacks destroy me.

A book discovered: *Nervous Christians.*
That's what I am: a nervous Christian!
I consume the book.
Need more faith, the author chides.
Trying to face my problems by myself;

need more humility. But I am praying
without ceasing; I am pleading, searching,
crying out to God. Humility? Must I lie prostrate
covering my head with sackcloth and ashes?
God does not hear, does not answer!

Now, not only depressed and fearful,
but also guilty for being depressed,
for being a nervous Christian.
The therapy sessions continue~
of little value. First item of business:

"You are six payments behind."
What do you expect: a new born baby,
going to college on borrowed money.
Second item: "How did your past week go?"
"My friend murdered his pregnant wife."

Is suicide the only way out of uncontrollable
depression? I fear, I fear I may lose control
of my actions as well as my thoughts.
Hide the knives and the bullets for my gun.
I no longer trust myself; I fear, I fear!

The diplomas conferred, I struggle
across the stage; mortar boards take wings.
The jubilant crowd suffocates me;
my stomach a hard knot.
My studies, once a crutch, now over.

What next? What now?
Panic stricken, I interview, and again,
before school boards with more
confidence in me than I have.
Before the classroom I stand,

knees drumming against my desk.
My students, attentive, bright-eyed, and eager.
Never had a frightened teacher before;
but they don't know about the
gut-retching anxiety behind the painted smile.

They like the new school,
they appear to enjoy their new teacher.
Lesson planning till sleep overcomes.
Routine builds confidence.
I begin to see beyond my fears.

A shaky recovery beginning?
My dry humor once lost resurfacing little
by little. I am cautious~will it last?
Self-confidence so shaky but growing.
I welcome the morning that I once dreaded.

Please, God, no more friends committing
suicide or murdering a pregnant wife,
uncontrolled behavior of demented minds
like real life Hitchcock.
Insanity, my greatest fear!

Regaining control of my thoughts
and emotions: no surprises, no
shocking news. The path out of depression
is neither fast nor without setbacks,
nor is it guaranteed.

Salvation is oblique, not coming
from God's hand reaching down,
but from the little hands that
surround me reaching out. They
came to learn, but offered salvation.

Train Whistle

Distant train whistle in the night;
your destinations many,
your journeys are long.
Your freedom an illusion,
controlled by man-made schedule,
constrained by ribbons of steel.

The illusion is appealing: freedom is ours,
we think~freedom of thought, freedom
to choose. But our thoughts, our ideas
are constrained, not free;
their breadth and travel restricted;
their destinations programmed.

Hard-wired by evolution,
soft-wired by parental expectations,
social mores, religious instruction.
Sidetracked by friends, teachers, circumstances.
How can we expand our journey, plan our own
schedules, choose our own destinations?

Just Wondering

Have I left a mark,
made a difference?
I often wonder.
Have I touched someone,
inspired anyone?

I would like to know.
But what device can measure?
Has my presence on earth
improved society, or has it been
all about me getting all I can?

Teacher: thirty-five years before the classroom.
Looking at those eager, innocent faces.
Did you reach their minds, inspire lifelong
learning, instill a thirst for knowledge?
Prepare them to recognize truth?

Preacher: thirty-five years behind the pulpit:
did you make a difference?
Do the congregates understand God's kingdom better,
Comprehend God's expectations more clearly?
What if your theology was wrong?

Missionary: a lifetime committed to Africa
preaching the Christian Gospel
and the American way of life to the natives.
Their spiritually often exceeded your own.
Could you have learned from them?

College professor: in the footsteps of Thoreau,
questioning society's infatuation with technology:
Challenging your students to question their choices,
to work for a better society; or was Thoreau wrong?
Or did your hypocrisies compromise your lectures?

Married: fifty years together,
through sickness and health, rich and poor.
Has it made a difference for both of you?
Have you helped each other grow,
enriched each other's life, experienced daily joy?

What is the measure of success?
What we achieve? What we accumulate?
To find joy in the common experiences of life?
To seek justice and practice compassion?
To help others become all they can be?

What does it mean,
to gain the whole world
but lose one's own soul? Did I see God
in the uninspired, the homely,
the redneck? Did they see God in me?

If our influence has been positive,
how long will it be carried forward:
a year, a generation, a lifetime?
If the influence was negative,
how long?

What If

If I had been raised in Mumbai,
would I have followed Gandhi?
If I had been born in South Africa,
on which side of apartheid would I have chosen?

If I was raised Roman Catholic,
would I have practiced birth control?
If I had been raised in Munich, would I
have joined Hitler's youth program?

If I had been born to an Indian squaw,
would I have left the reservation and gone to college?
If I had grown up in our town, not in the country
would I have married the country girl I did?

If my father had been a preacher,
would I have become a missionary, or a rebel?
If I had been born in a large city,
would I have joined a gang?

If I had been born a woman, would I
have become a women's lib advocate and not married?
Or would I have become a subordinate wife?
or a lesbian?

If I had been born Southern Baptist,
would I now believe that God created it all
in six days and planted fossils to distract me?
Or would I be a closet evolutionist?

If I had majored in literature in college
instead of industrial technology
would I have become a writer
and not the CEO of a company?

If I had not been raised Mennonite,
would I still be opposed to war
as a solution to international problems,
or would I have joined the Army?

Chance Meeting #1:
Man of Letters

Kurt Vonnegut, guest at Wichita State.
"Do you believe in abortion?"
the young man inquired.
"Oh, are you pregnant?" Vonnegut replied.
"Next question."

Chance Meeting #2:
The Retired Professor

I met him between the organic oats
and the seven-grain bread mix.
How old are you? He inquired.
74, I replied.

I'm 84, said he proudly.
I still have my hair, doffing his cap,
revealing a few silver strands.
I knew him well.

What is your occupation? He asked.
I taught at the local college, said I.
Well, so did I! he answered.
He knew me well back then.

Do you want the oat bran ground finer?
The clerk inquired.
What did my wife write
on the note? Said he.

Chance Meeting #3:
The Ghana Tailor

Huge red and yellow flowers adorned her
flowing dress, tailored for her ample body.
No doubt sewn in her own miniscule factory:
four seamstresses in the outskirts of the capital city.
She, effervescent, expressing daily her love for life.
Fluent in English and a native dialect,
now a guest of the American Information Agency,
learning computer generated pattern-making
and principles of international marketing.
How was it that she also spoke fluent German?

We Americans with our one-language monologue.

Chance Meeting #4:
The Luster

How are you coping, old man? I ask.
I'm struggling with the commandment on lusting,
he replied: Thou shalt not lust after your
neighbor's wife. I wonder, does God
disapprove of my lusting after my own wife?
She thinks I'll get over it with age,
but I'm 95 now.

Chance Meeting #5:
The Hoarder

His fleet: three cars, three pickups;
two startable, one drivable~barely.
Fender dents, door nicks,
sagging bumpers, rattling tailpipes~
history of former lives.

Four-door Chevy,
one available seat;
remainder inundated with
last year's mail, soiled jacket,
auction fliers six months yellow.

A check for an oil lease out the
window, freed by the Kansas wind,
making its way to Omaha.
(He claims that he never received it.)
The dash, an annexed tool store:

pliers, screwdrivers, pipe wrench,
grease-streaked shop rags,
blocking the windshield.
The dining table once dark oak,
now inches deep collage of

newspapers and invoices~
due and overdue,
handled multiple times.
A cluttered mind;
A cluttered life;

When Did It Happen?

Like every newly wed,
we looked to our parents.
We vowed, ours will be different.
We will grow together,
like a spring breeze caressing
flowers into full bloom.

No arguments about who will be first;
no blame, no guilt, no negatives.
Love will prevail.
What happened along the way?
Was ours really no different?
When did we quit choosing each other?

When did "we" become "I"?
When did "lover" become simply "spouse"?
When did "our" time become "my" time?
When did passion give way to duty
and romance to household chores?
After pabulum and toilet training?

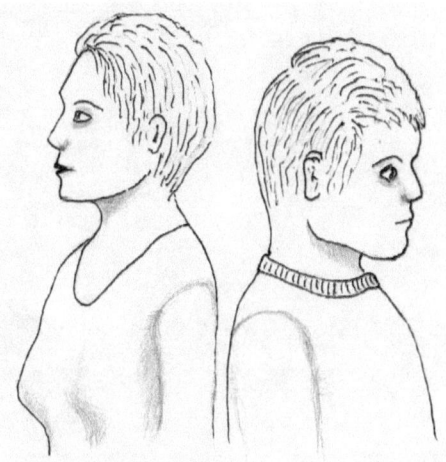

When graduate school called?
When my career demanded my attention?
When did acceptance and support
evolve into criticism. When did
communication begin to break down?
When did forgiveness become defensiveness?

When did touching and holding shift from
being desirable to being an annoyance?
When did "I'm sorry" slip from our
vocabulary? Was our love lost to selfishness
or due to lack of attention?

Born to Work

God has no use for the lazy, the indolent,
the idle, the sluggish, the slacker.
When did hard work become
synonymous with salvation?

I was raised to shun personal pleasures,
a pattern established by ancestors in Europe,
continued in the southern Ukraine,
a work ethic admired by Catherine the Great.

My forefathers honored God by their work.
Pleasures were a distraction from honoring God.
Jesus, their model, a carpenter, never
succumbed to earthly pleasure, or did he?

Never danced to the flute and lyre?
Never wrote poetry for pleasure?
Never attended concerts by the great masters?
Never fly-fished for St. Peter's fish in the Jordan?

Never collected paintings or pottery?
Never played on the Jerusalem Sluggers?
Did not own a wardrobe of fashionable robes?
Was his life as austere as we imagine?

Did he travel to the Far East to study
Buddhism, as some speculate? Did he ever
travel for pleasure to learn about Greek and
Roman mythology, the early Chinese dynasties?

Does the Protestant work ethic really
have anything to do with Spirituality?
Are personal pleasures really an abomination,
a distraction from experiencing God?

The Odd Couple

They were the unlikely couple.
He, tattered straw hat resting on protruding ears,
sweat-stained dark around the band;
week's stubble on a pockmarked face,
leathered by a half century
under the scalding Kansas sun;
graying hair frizzed on the back of his neck
in need of the quarterly barber shop visit;
Hand-rolled cigarette dangling from scaly lips;
overalls threadbare at the knees
above high-top cracked leather.

She, slender as a New York model.
Black hair cascading to her pinched waist,
high cheek bones framing smiling brown eyes.
Full, crimson lips above a petite chin.
Her skin—smooth, tan; no evidence
of hard work or hardship.
Two children between them:
boy, a Huck Finn type—hers;
young girl, carbon of her mother—theirs.

What drew her to him,
20 years her senior on a rundown farm.
Was it desperation for the young divorcee?
Need for security and stability?
How did he court her?
What promises did he have to make?
What was the chemistry?
Do opposites really attract?

Citizen of the Field

I was a citizen of the field.
I knew the sweet smell of cut alfalfa; the stink
of steaming cow manure in the milk barn.
The musty odor of mice and rats in the granary;
the fragrant aroma of turned soil after harvest;
the stinging essence of spilled
gasoline when fueling the tractor.
The stench of the outdoor privy,
the nauseating odor of a skunk
surprised in the barn; the
mouth-watering aroma of roast beef
straight from the wood-burning range.

I was a citizen of the field.
In the dim light of a kerosene lamp, I read
Old Yeller and worked fourth-grade arithmetic.
In the field, I shouted "Giddap." Prince and Nell,
masters of a two-word vocabulary,
lurched forward to the next oat shock, "Whoa."
I skinned the steer, stuffed pork sausage,
plucked the feathers off butchered chickens.

I was a citizen of the field.
Inundated by a cloud of insects seeking
tractor lights, I plowed the field
in the darkness of night to avoid the
Kansas sun and the searing southwest wind;
walked circles forty feet up,
packing chopped corn in the
neighbor's silo, wishing for a guard rail.

I was a citizen of the field
until Soren Kierkegaard, Emile Durkheim,
and Robert Frost beckoned. Or was it
Willa Cather, Herman Melville, and Karl Sagan
who called me in from the field?

Ah, Youth

Ah, the idealism of youth!
We anticipated the perfect world
where national leaders respected
the boundaries of their neighbors;
where all life was considered sacred;
where governments looked after the most
vulnerable and marginalized among us;
where corporations did not rape
the masses and the environment
but had a philanthropic conscience;
where Congress worked for the good
of the people, not for their re-election.

Where is the anger of my youth
when I saw society devoid of love
and compassion, where selfishness and
greed prevailed? Where is the outrage
that filled my soul as I observed
redneck hate, racial profiling
and gender inequalities?
When indignation over government
decisions to declare war prompted me
to participate in protest rallies, peace
marches, and letter-writing campaigns?

Have I grown complacent, too
preoccupied with my life to care?
Are my concerns no longer about
the injustices in society?
Am I so engrossed in extending my life
instead of the lives of others; too

focused on fulfilling my bucket list?
Do I now willingly accept the *status quo*,
believing that attitudes and laws are too
difficult to change, forgetting that
Martin Luther King, Jr., Rosa Parks,
and a bunch of Wichita high school
kids made it happen?

What happened to the idealism
and anger of my youth?
Am I now just another uninvolved,
inactive American citizen?

Truths Learned Along the Way

That my future is unpredictable despite my efforts to control it.

That time goes faster when you need it, and drags when you're waiting.

That my life would hold so many opportunities for creativity and joy but not the time nor the resolve to embrace them all.

That habits of impatience and anger are so difficult to break.

That Einstein was correct when he said, "Life is like riding a bicycle: if you quit moving forward, you'll fall down."

That I would never have it all together when I became an adult the way I thought my parents did.

That my priorities in retirement would be so difficult to complete.

That marriage would require so many compromises.

That when my spouse says "don't bother" she may really mean "please do."

That not speaking my feelings is often the best path.

That my children would teach me so much.

That how I respond to my spouse and children may be more important than what I say.

That my adult children aren't interested in my advice as much as they welcome my labor and support.

That I agonize too much about things I cannot change.

That everyone I love will eventually die.

That my wife and I must plan to grow old together, or we will grow old apart.

That the red meat we grew on the farm was not good for me.

Someone who doesn't read is little better off than someone who cannot read.

That absolute power controlled by one political party too often leads to deception and corruption.

That the political party of my father, a poor wheat farmer, favored the rich and big business.

That a country's leader could order six million people killed.

That the fatigue one Saturday morning would lead to open heart surgery.

That the hard hit in football would cause seizures thirty years later.

That God does not answer prayer, at least not on my timetable, but I am responsible for explaining why.

That heaven and hell are experienced on earth primarily caused by our own decisions.

That right action is more important than "right" theology.

That religion and god are human constructs, since humans cannot contemplate nonexistence and want a hell for those who were evil on earth. Yet a congregation, if not exclusive and judgmental, can be a supportive community, sharing joys and sorrows.

That the writer, like the artist, is least qualified to judge his own work.

That, in my lifetime, man would walk on the moon.

That the United States would be the first to develop a weapon capable of wiping out the whole human race--and use it!

That cockroaches, termites, and ants are forever, humans are not.

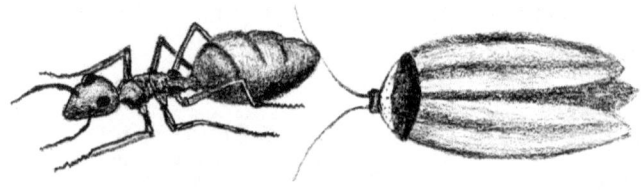

When the Grandchildren Leave

Re-vacuum the house—the whole house.
Flush the stools—all of them, twice.
Dump the water out of the soap dishes.
Search for the shampoo bottle.
Wipe the yellow spots off the wall and
floor tile around the bathroom stools.
Scrub the footprints off the playroom walls.
Wipe the jelly stains from around the light switches.
Take the storm door to the hardware store
to have the screen re-stretched.
Re-roll the toilet tissue and
put it back on the roller.
Repair the keyboard cover on the piano
that was pulled out too far.
Wash the mud off the garage floor
where the kids made mud pies.
Replace the Gold Spot Euonymus
beside the driveway, victim of bicycle traffic.
Remove the ketchup stains on the
upholstered living room chairs.
Fill the dings in the new maple floor
with wood putty.

Call the grandkids, tell them
how much you enjoyed their visit,
and ask when they can come again!

American Culture

Accident of Birth

We do not choose our parents,
place of birth;
color of skin,
our ancestry.

You were born in a thatched hut.
Like many of us,
an accident of passion.
Your skin is ebony.

Education, an unfulfilled dream.
No chance to learn a trade.
Your future predetermined.
But you are loved.

You spend your youth
fetching water from the village well,
searching for fuel, digging manioc.
Drawing pictures in the dirt.

You bear your firstborn; the cycle repeats.
No chance to witness other cultures
to see Paris, visit Fifth Avenue.
No chance to read the great philosophers.

No need for a nervous breakdown.
You know who you are, where you belong.
The sun rises; the sun sets.
Survival is your skill.

I was born in the United States
with pale skin, Germanic ancestry.
Not in a hut,
not in a ghetto.

I am privileged.
Choices are mine: education, occupation,
private transportation, travels,
mode of communication.

We are obsessed with our health:
trans fats, calories, hypertension.
Bodies examined by radiation, ultrasound,
magnetic fields, probes.

We are obsessive:
addicted to latest technology.
Restaurant tabs that would feed your village;
storage units for unneeded possessions.

We are obsessed with our possessions:
two cars and SUV in the drive,
cabin cruiser at the dock
five credit cards maxed.

Obsessed with our personal image:
liposucked thighs, collagen-filled lips,
silicon-enhanced breasts, artificially-induced tans.
Yet, an obesity epidemic for lack of discipline.

Dominated by stress and depression,
we search for meaning: drugs, therapy,
self-fulfillment seminars,
possessions, weekend retreats.

Manifest Destiny

Manifest destiny is ours, you say.
But by what measure have we been chosen by God
to police the world, to impose our economic system,
our mode of government and our religion on all?

We who destroyed the native habitat of those
who preceded us; killing their food source,
herding them like cattle to worthless lands~
Are we fit to lead the world?

We who brought slaves to these shores to pick
our cotton, till our fields, provide sexual pleasure for
their masters, then deprived them of their unalienable rights~
Are we fit to lead the world?

We who, with four percent of the world's population
consume 25% of the consumed nonrenewable fuels
in our power plants, vehicles, stadium lights~
Are we fit to lead the world?

We who pollute the air, water, and soil, and contribute
to global warming with no thought for preserving
the environment for future generations~
Are we fit to lead the world?

We who place monetary wealth, entertainment,
and conspicuous consumption above meeting
basic human needs of those with limited means~
Are we fit models for the world?

We who give bonuses to the rich as they foreclose
on the homes of those who are unemployed,
who must choose medicine over mortgage payments–
Are we fit models for the world?

We with the highest gun death rate of civilized nations;
but believe that concealed weapons for all
and capitol punishment are deterrents to crime–
Are we fit to lead the world?

We who hold suspected war criminals in prison
without the right to trial, and use methods
of interrogation classified as torture by others–
Are we fit to lead the world?

We who import doctors and engineers
because our public education system lacks
the challenges and opportunities to equip our young–
Are we fit to lead the world?

We who have an obesity and diabetes epidemic
because of our fast-food industry, and
a self-indulgent, sedentary lifestyle–
Are we fit models for the world?

We who consider our country to be a land of
tolerance and fairness, yet still discriminate in the
workplace based on gender, race, and sexual orientation–
Are we fit models for other societies?

We who champion an economic system
that rewards, empowers, and protects the
rich while disenfranchising the expanding poor~
Are we fit to lead the world?

We whose ancestors immigrated from Europe
but now mistreat and deport those who, like us,
want to follow their dreams in this country~
Are we fit to lead the world?

We who were the first to create a nuclear bomb, and
use it indiscriminately to kill 140,000 innocent people,
with enough reserve now to annihilate the world's population~
Are we safe to lead the world?

We who consider ourselves to be religious,
and believe it gives us the right to judge others, ignoring
the widow, the sick, the hungry, the poor, the homeless~
Are we fit models for the world?

May we see the arrogance of our attitudes;
in humility, may we become creators of a healthier,
more just, more compassionate, more sustainable world
for generations who will follow us.

D.C.

Yes, I've been to D.C.
White majestic columns;
straight, strong, majestic columns.
Abe, in solemn kindness and pity
studying the human chain
waiting to climb the steps to touch him,
and sobbing at the Vietnam wall.

I've been to D.C.
Reuben, McCormick, Monet, Whitney.
Fantastic models seeking protection.
Touch football and gulls on the mall;
Lindbergh's Spirit suspended, Redskins.
Stepping over faceless souls
clutching subway vents.

I've been to D.C.
Arrogance of power in the chambers.
Hopelessness of the powerless on the streets.
Georgetown mansion splendor.
Vertical slum pathos, passing powder in the alley.
Champagne, dim lights, mood music.
I've been to D.C.

The Congregation

In clerical collar he sits, waiting his moment,
randomly scanning the faces before him.
What is he thinking?

Scares me to death to get up in front of these people.
Fifteen retired, ordained ministers out there.

The whole congregation is a shade of gray.
How can we attract more young people?

Oh, yes! Helen ought to quit choir! She always flats.
But what can you do if you have a volunteer choir?

There sit Karl and Emma. Should I be so lucky as to have
my grandson take me to church when I'm 90!

Why don't the Jezels take their bawling baby to the
nursery? Every Sunday I can hear him from here.

Old J. J., worth a couple million, the old miser!
Won't give a penny to the building fund.

God, look at all those widows, and there are two in the
homes for every one here.

I hate doing funerals. Hard to be honest while making
everyone a saint.

What do we do with Elizabeth, always wants to help.
Tries to scare the devil out of the little kids.
Too conservative for our Sunday School!

Hope Russ doesn't snore out loud during the sermon again.

The scripture reading completed, he rises, walks slowly to the podium, arranges his notes, looks across the congregation~his congregation, as if for the first time:

"Dearly beloved . . . . . ."

Recession American Style

"Buy!" says the government.
"Consume!" say the merchants.
"Spend!" say the Democrats.
"The only way out!" say the Republicans.
"Earn Reward Points!" say the credit card companies.
"Unsustainable!" says Howard Zinn.

Human Evolution

Homo Technos, a species evolved
from 21st century *Homo sapiens* (an indigenous
species), but choosing a synthetic world proudly
developed by their own assumed cleverness.

Forests replaced by shopping malls;
clover fields given way to clover leafs and thruways.
Meadow grasses, harbinger of the seasons,
now replaced by monochromatic perennial green

dissected by ribbons of concrete;
trees installed according to an urban code
that discriminates against indigenous species.
Flower beds of genetically-modified flora.

Face to face communication once prevalent
among the natives now carried worldwide
riding electronic waves
available to all who care to listen.

Friend and neighbor dialog once experienced
by proximity over the backyard fence,
bridge and pinochle matches, block parties
now restricted to a declining subculture.

E-mailing, texting, blogging, Facebook, twitter;
vocabulary, grammar and spelling modified.
Face-to-face communication an inferior means;
personal identity, security compromised.

Culture redefined; art and music
mediated by technology: everyone an artist,
everyone a "talented" composer.
Genius is compromised

When technology mediates, the artist
replaced by the technician.
the artist's brush no longer
touches the canvas.

Sandlot ballgames,
walks in the forest
exchanged for the mesmerizing screen.
Physical activity compromised.

Strangers from different times,
different lands meet on the screen.
Deception becomes *status quo*;
Truth and reality compromised.

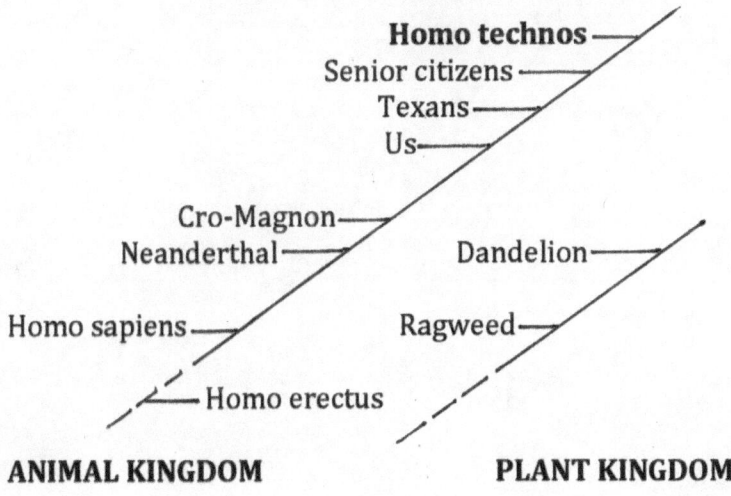

Computer graphics converts lines
and planes into visual animatable objects
that do not exist. Solid modeling
converts visual depictions into solid reality.

Time now measured in nanoseconds.
Communication never fast enough.
Speed, the marker of quality.
Quality replaced by quantity.

Technology~something gained;
something lost.
Technology, said Thoreau,
a better means to a no better end.

Student Union

Lady with the big RED STAR on
your sweats, what's that book in your
hands? Marx? Begin? You part of the cult?
Just like stars and moons?

You at the faculty table,
surrounded by student melee, glaringly visible.
Worsted brown tweed; double Windsor tie;
eyeglasses perched amidst curly brown
turning gray, focused skyward.

Hey! ROTC man,
Did you fall for that free tuition
stuff? "You learn to kill,
we'll pay your bill." Or
did you just want free hair cuts?

HIGH-TECH WOMAN: long-chain molecule
eye lashes, Chemical tan, polyester shimmer
over silicon, throbbing mechanically
to wired-in environs. "How Cooool."
Your digitizer needs adjusting.

Hey, BIG MAN:
How long you been lifting weights?
Biceps plus ACT score, you qualified!
We NEED YOU!
Are you also taking classes?

Our eyes meet.
Our minds are suddenly linked in that
moment of uncontrollable, steaming passion.
Differences in age, background vanish;
What is this magic chemistry?

The big screen mesmerizes, tantalizes;
I gather my books, make my way to the door.

Modern Deity

God is passé, irrelevant.
We are too busy pursuing
life to think about life after life.
We have no need for God.

To the contrary. We immerse ourselves
daily in the sacred. Not the God of the temple,
the church, the synagogue; more real, more
visible, more reliable, more responsive.

Prayer shawls, bended knee, raised hands, beads~archaic,
obsolete. Truly, our God is with us to the ends of the earth.
Omnipresent, in the tallest skyscraper, the smallest pixel,
in the space station, on the trail, 20,000 leagues below.

Yea, though we walk through the valley
of death, we need fear no natural enemy.
Our God will supply our every need to our
extended end. Death, where is your victory?

Our deity encompasses; no, replaces all others~
Mohammed, Allah, the Buddha, the Christ.
All powerful, omnipotent, giver of life, delayer
of death. Other gods acquiesce in the face of the tangible.

Truth is revealed; no need to gaze through
a glass darkly. Life is amplified, magnified,
demystified, DNAified; indispensable, our god:
Technology!

Night Watch

The others were breathing noisily,
their ears as closed as their minds.
I was still awake sensing something
in this strange place.

The sounds of night--the dishwasher
on the floor below: rrr-shs, rrr-shs, rrr-shs.
The thud of the furnace as the fan jerked alive,
The hot water heater breathing.

But that noise in the alley.
A peek through the blinds--nothing.
But it was something!
A cat in the dumpster?

A dog after a rat?
The wind moving its belongings?
New gang graffiti
on the far wall?

Someone jiggling the padlock
on the gate? It was something.
I crawled under the covers,
closed my eyes and slept.

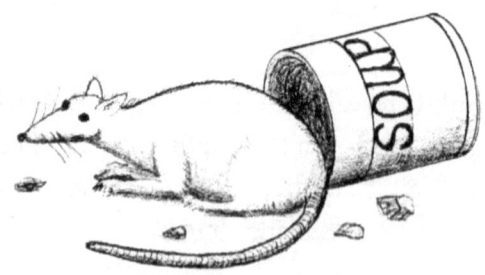

Ode to America

O, tis Country Time on the Plaza;
    White Cloud, White Rain above, Selsun Blue everywhere.
Advil and Mary Kay eloped that Summer Eve,
    Possessed as they were by Obsession and Lust.

O, this night of Sominex and NyQuil;
    Where is your sleeplessness?
Breakfast of Frosted Cakes, Frosted Flakes, and Frosted Hair,
    Where are your nutrients?

O, vanity of Cutex, Avon, and Cover Girl;
    Where is your face?
Don your Spandex, Stridex, and Playtex
    and forget not your Pentax!

O, great Mydol, Preparation H, and Nuprin;
    Where, o where is your pain?
Slip into your Orlon, Ban Lon, and Hanes
    And then Roll-On.

O, Jolly Green Giant, provider of every Dry Idea;
    Where are your Froot-Loops?
And where are Advil and Mary Kay?
    Are they Soft-N-Dri or has Advil seduced the Minute Maid?

O, great Roach Motel,
    Armed with MegaCaps, Stresstabs, and Exlax,
Let us Aim for a Fresh Start and obtain Sheer Elegance
    Full of Cheer and Bartles and Jaymes.

Successful Men

The Magazine of Successful Men,
but I'm not in it.
The editor doesn't know about me.
I'm not the CEO of anything,
a Hollywood star, a home-run king.

Only a college professor
wearing tweeds and frumpy sweaters.
But I have a different tie for every day
of the semester. Surely that
is significant~or maybe not.

But many successful men I know
are not in the magazine.
My father who lost everything in the Depression
but retired comfortably~that's success!
Or my uncle, the Chicago cop,

who avoided corruption,
and never fired his gun in 35 years,
except in target practice
where he aimed at the hands and
feet of the silhouetted image.

Or the successful farming neighbor
in Kansas for whom I walked circles
in a silo forty feet off the ground without a rail
packing chopped corn. He was successful
(until he hanged himself in the barn).

Editor, how about a magazine
of successful men who died of suicide?
Or a magazine of successful men
whose lives ended in mental institutions,
or who died early of whiskey poisoning?

Or successful men who abused
their wives and spanked their kids, or picked up
boy prostitutes in the park north of the Loop?
Or never put money into the Salvation Army kettle?
Now those would make interesting magazines!

Meaning of Life

College student, self-assured, invincible.
In suspended animation; adult,
yet not fully. The assignment:
explain the meaning of life.
Elucidate your beliefs and values.

Intellectualization, so important,
yet the big questions of life are
pondered, not in the classroom,
but at 2:30 a.m. when the baby cries;
when your spouse is diagnosed with cancer,

when looking into your mother's coffin;
when awaiting a liver transplant
that will never come.
Life consists of dreams fulfilled,
dreams unrealized, of compromises,

often beyond our control.
You will realize that you cannot
turn back the clock
to relive mistakes you've made.
So, college student,

explain the meaning of life.
Explore her depths. Compose
the perfect essay; satisfy the
assignment. Then commence,
begin the process in the flesh.

Class Reunion

I remember you well, but
you've changed: that family nose,
a distinguishing characteristic,
no longer distinguishing.

Did you look in the mirror and say,
"I don't like what I see"?
Did someone say, "Quite a nose you have"?
(You weren't really unattractive before.)

(Others in our class had more
to gain from a facelift than you!)
You requested we address you
"Katherine," no longer "Katie".

A total make-over?
No, the voice has not changed.
Still the same ol' Katie.
But your appearance . . .

Did you alter your thinking also,
or has conservatism kept its ground?
Did you switch political parties? Did
conservative Katie become liberal Katherine?

The Burning Question:
will this be the permanent you,
or will you tire of the new you
and modify again?

Just War

One night in World War II,
England and America burned 25,000
German citizens to death
and displaced 200,000 more,
citizens guilty of living in Dresden.

Two atomic bombs, courtesy of the USA,
annihilated 140,000 Japanese citizens,
millions more exposed to an epidemic
of cancer, citizens guilty of living
in Nagasaki and Hiroshima.

Hitler murdered six million Jews
and persecuted countless more,
guilty of having the wrong ancestry,
victims of an anti-Semitic myth.

Hitler and we were proud of these murders,
our ability to destroy families like our own;
children whose parents loved them;
children with a bright future, until. . . .

How do we justify such destruction of humanity?
Is not compassion the highest virtue?
War is now sophisticated.
Innocent citizens no longer targets,

yet terrorists strike indiscriminately,
targeting the busy marketplace,
genocide still practiced; hospitals, schools,
homes, collateral damage from errant missiles.

Culture and history is obliterated.
Rational thought, ours and theirs, destroyed.
The enemy, considered an inferior species,
disposable objects, like Styrofoam coffee cups,
below us in intelligence and culture.

The enemy, guilty for living inside
the wrong borders, led by a power-hungry leader
seeking infamy, having wrong ancestry
or skin color, following the wrong god.

We, guilty of prejudice and retaliation;
Manipulated by political leaders
wanting to leave a legacy,
believers in a manifest destiny myth.

We, succumbing to irrational rhetoric
and political propaganda.
We, victims of national pride.
Actions justified with old religion rationale.

When will we ever learn the sanctity of life?
When will we ever learn
no such thing as a just war.

Fears—A List Poem

American society, a fear-based society. We fear much.

Electrical shorts and sinkholes
Gray hair and drive-by shootings
Credit card theft and heart attacks
Terrorists and mad cow disease
Pharmacy errors and flat chests
Alzheimer's disease and break-ins
Open manholes and lead pipe plumbing
Strokes and Monday mornings
Wrinkled skin and letter bombs
Speeding tickets and brown spiders
Falling elevators and clogged stools
High places and pit bulls
Drug reactions and mice in the house
Killer bees and tight places
Growing old and collapsing bridges
Sounds in the night and taxes
Rabid skunks and road map veins
Lab reports and large birds
Bacteria and drunk drivers
Obesity and airplane crashes
Deer ticks and artificial sweeteners
Court summons and overdrafts
Suicide bombers and internal parasites
Termites and The Flu
Radio waves and hard-drive crashes
Tornados and asbestos
Lawsuits and cancer
Diarrhea and radical fundamentalists
Snakes and underarm deodorants

Paint fumes and head lice
Aluminum pans and viruses
Fire ants and snipers
Sleep apnea and AK 47's
Rapists and macular degeneration
Erectile dysfunction and arthritis
Earth quakes and pitch darkness
Morning sickness and deafness
Getting fired and pedophiles
Government surveillance and Congress
God and death.

Tributes and End Time

Time

Time, relentless time.
You accelerate the sunset
and crawl in the waiting room.
You pass swiftly during passion,
but prolong my pain.
I cannot control you.

Time, relentless time.
We are children, parents,
then grandparents.
We go to school, we work, we retire.
Eager youngsters take our places,
sit at our desks, plow our fields.

Time passes swiftly but silently,
a wind-driven cloud in the night,
but a dark cloud that
hovers over the healthcare unit.

I'm Going to Die

Maybe not today, but I don't know.
Reminded often.
Friends on the obituary page,
funerals, memorial services~people my age.
Visits to the cemetery on Memorial Day.
Evangelicals warning, "Prepare to meet your God."
Estate planners hawking: "Plan to meet your mortician.
Prepare a will~avoid probate. Put it all in writing."

What should I discard as I downsize in preparation:
collector's magazines saved these many years~
Kennedy assassinations, man on the moon;
Martin Luther King, Jr.'s dream?
My publications, dissertation, UNESCO speech
My Power Point presentations, my library?
Who gets my son's still lifes (given with love),
the dining room set crafted from the black walnut
on my wife's childhood home, the Regier prints?

Who should get my body?
the earth? a canister? a lab?
Medical students poking and jabbing:
(or is it joking and grabbing).
My freshly repaired heart~no longer leaking,
but a leaky esophagus and bladder,
watery eyes, broken nose,
full head of hair, dusty white,
flat feet.

But what is it like to die? What if it's sudden?
a stroke, aneurysm, 18 wheeler.
Is there a special pain in dying?
worse than a tooth extraction or the stomach flu?
What if I have five minutes to think before I go:
my wife, will she have to sell the house?
who will rub her back? My children:
how will they finish remodeling their houses
without me? How will they celebrate
Father's Day?

What if death comes slowly?
How will it be when I can no longer
hear the cardinal sing?
If I can't sculpt or write? Can't walk
or see? If my thinking is confused,
won't I wish for death? Will they
prolong death, IV tubes, 20 pills a day,
forcing me to stay alive when
I am no longer myself?
Shouldn't that be criminal?

What will I feel as I leave my body?
Nirvana? Nothing?
Relief from earthly pain, from
house payments, rising gas prices, taxes?
Whom will I meet as life slips away?
Jesus? Saint Peter? The other guy with the horns?
Mom and Pop? My favorite uncle?
My deceased pastor? Nobody?

What will I see as life leaves me?
A band of angels singing Handel's Hallelujah
chorus? (a Dixieland band, I hope, dirgefully
playing, "When the Saints Come Marching in.")
Streets paved with gold? Baptist Avenue,
Mennonite Alley, Muslim Boulevard? What?
Special quarters for those who healed
the sick, fed the hungry, housed the
homeless, visited the prisoner, clothed the
naked, made peace, showed love to all?

If I'm reincarnated,
do I get to choose my next body? Next
nationality? (I hope not Chinese, its a tough
language.) If I don't choose, who does?
How will I know I've been reincarnated?
How will I know I've died?
Will I be out-of-body watching myself die?
Will I be able to view life on earth after death?
Or does the system shut down
immediately and completely?

Are there no instruction manuals?
No crib notes for the final exam?
No *Death for Dummies*?
I'm not ready to die just yet:
The list of things I must do on the house
and yard is still two pages long, small font,
single-spaced. My wife expects me to finish
them before I go! Should I look forward
to death? I don't know death, I only know life.

The Hunting Dog

Fossilized in the porch corner,
brown muzzle turned white;
he rises slowly, stretches arthritic limbs.
Circles the mat, slumps down once more.

Ten years ago, the ad stated:
"Hunting dog: small, brown, friendly, loyal.
Faster than a rabbit, quick as a cat."
Ten years ago.

A car rattles past on the gravel road.
One solitary bark~delayed; feeble attempt
to protect the estate. No more biting
at the rotating rubber at 30 miles per hour.

The master's tractor coughs to life!
Suddenly awake; ears erect.
Limps from the porch, following the sound,
responding to memories of earlier conquests.

No longer hears the dickcissel.
Blurred eyes no longer see the rabbits
escaping the mower blades.
Content to trot along, tongue tasting the air.

The stooped man in the nursing home
a born leader, voted most likely to succeed;
graduated with an MBA, summa cum laude,
ran marathons, authored books on leadership.

Now fossilized in a recliner, his hair,
silver as a tarnished dime. No longer hears
the flute or the warbler. Eyes fixed on the blurred
screen, sounds and images he cannot comprehend.

No longer stimulated by intellectual discourse
nor lifted by a Vivaldi concert.
His successes only a fading memory now.
He asks, "Why am I here?"

What Really Matters?

Age 41, the perfect picture of robust health,
enjoying every minute of life.
Four years of college football,
building muscles, crushing opponents.
Now a super salesman,
the symbol of success and exuberance.

He loved his beautiful wife and
excited his two children with
clever surprises and special treats.
His friends, often on the receiving end
of his practical jokes, enjoyed his
company, his humor, his zest for life.

But then an ache in his midsection
became persistent. Tests revealed
intestinal cancer~an uncommon
disease for an uncommon lover of life.
"I'll beat it," he said with teethed clenched,
"just as I've beat every other challenge!"

Denial, so common for the young and
diseased, was his response.
His smile did not fade; his
love of life was not diminished.
He cheered his son's football games,
attended his wife's social functions.

But the pain became excruciating.
Three months later the cancer won:
the one opponent he could not lick!
Sitting in the pew I ponder.
Life is unpredictable,
full of surprises, some without options.

If I had known that I would live only 17 years, or 41,
what would have really mattered to me?
How would I have lived my life differently?
What would I have wanted to experience before I died?
How would my day-to-day behavior been different?
How would I have valued relationships?

Would I have argued about the
insignificant? Would have defending my
opinions dominated my personality?
Would making a name for myself
have been my highest goal?
Whatever really matters?

Whatever is most important,
I should be practicing it daily, since
I don't know when the bell
will toll for me.

High School Fullback

High school culture: passing notes in English;
distorted faces in algebra, suppressing
laughter behind the teacher's back;
tripping freshmen in the halls.

Jamming lockers full of smelly gym clothes.
Victoria's Secret on someone's monitor.
"Accidentally" bumping into female gender.
Sports convocations: "We will, we will rock you ...."

High school, discovering oneself, others.
Discovering talents and interests;
discovering what you are, and what you're not.
What you can be; what you won't be.

High school activities: history term papers,
snapping jock straps in the locker room,
debate contests, drums. Plans for the future:
summer camp, vocation, a serious fiancé.

His father's handgun, held to his temple.
The future ended. No more self discovery.
The fullback~no more fulfilling a father's dream,
or responding to a mother's love.

Friends, classmates stunned, sobered, puzzled.
Young man with a future, most likely to . . .
How could he do this to himself?
Why? With his whole future ahead?

A selfish act? An act of defiance?
A reaction to "what"?
A parent's disapproval of a girl friend?
Rumors. Only rumors.

A vacant seat in the van.
Empty chair at the dinner table.
Open slot in the backfield.
Silent drumsticks.

Parents in mourning and anguish.
Sixteen years of nurturing, caring, instructing.
The Priest, purveyor of forgiveness: "Don't blame yourselves."
Not a word about the soul in the coffin.

At Peace

June 9, 1911 - March 6, 2009

1:00 a.m.
Going on 98, but you won't make it.
The oxygen pump hisses and breathes.
Your eyes closed, your mouth open,
your breathing labored.

Do you understand what is happening?
You don't talk, can't talk;
no energy to form words.

You've refused food for four weeks now.
Yet your heart remained strong.
But that ominous gurgling sound
with every breathe . . .

The boom box on the side table, resonates quietly
like the sound track of a tent meeting, pleading:
"Are you washed in the blood,
in the precious blood of the lamb?"

1:30 a.m.
The oxygen level drops from 83% to 55%.
Your temperature has risen to 106 degrees.
Heart pumping at 112 bpm.
"What a friend we have in Jesus . . . ."

1:45 a.m.
Your daughter calls, "Come."
We all came, ignoring the speed limit.
Do you know we are all here
surrounding your bed?

Our gazes are fixed on you, yet empty,
but our minds full~pondering the meaning
of your 90 plus years.
How you raised us.

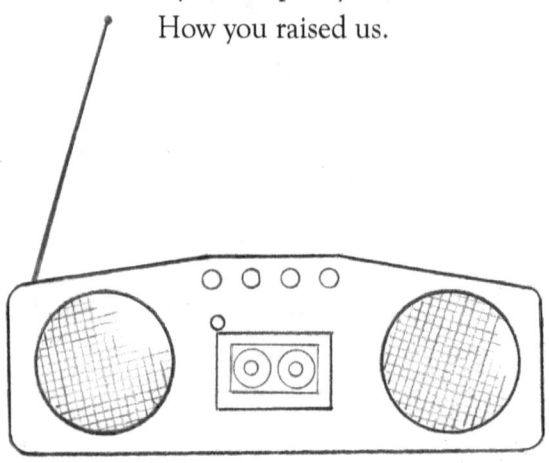

What you taught us,
how you influenced our values.
How your perspectives and ours differed
at times; but you loved us.

6:20 a.m.
Your chest heaves slightly~once, twice, thrice~
but not enough. It is over.
The annoying gurgle has stopped.
You are at peace; we will struggle on.

Thinking about My Brother

October 25, 1932-September 14, 2009

Our life is a composition, a symphony.
From the womb with random notes
but no melody, no pattern;
our music a work in progress,
ongoing as long as we breathe.
Others help or hinder,
want us to follow their melody,
sing their song, copy their genre`.
But what is **our** song?
Our place in the universe?
Our potential contribution, large or small?
That unique tune that will bring **us** fulfillment?

You, brother, wrote your piece
like the rest of us, one movement at a time
but were stopped short unexpectedly
in the middle of the final movement.
Born in SE Colorado in 1932, your prelude
not of your choosing, was simple,
covered with the dust of the '30's.
You and I shared that part of your symphony,
plowing fields, singing duets to the milk cows.

You began composing the next movement
in Denver where you helped restore
the melodies of others at St. Jo's Hospital.
Your marriage to Elsa, the nurse,
a crescendo in this movement
Your middle years together:
a pastoral symphony with Swiss overtones.

But within this movement
your life took an unusual turn:
you found your unique voice,
your music became literal:
three decades of singing praises to your Lord.
Faith Encounter inspired the music of others,
awakened their chords.

In your last movement, you left the cold winters,
sought a warmer climate, a new venue.
You were scheduled to sing in the Christmas pageant.
But the tolling bell sounded,
not anticipated, not in your planning.
Does your life remain an unfinished symphony
or was this abrupt ending the grand finale?
The maestro now gone,
but your composition lingers on,
bringing joy to all who knew you.

Staring at the Urn

My husband, dead.
Massive heart attack, they said.
Found him lying in the yard, the garden hose
still trickling, waiting for the pizza.

Why did you go first?
Me in my wheelchair, awaiting death.
How could you do this to me?
It isn't right, isn't fair.

For fifty-four years you gave me
your full, undivided attention.
Then my stroke. I needed
you more than ever.

You made my meals,
helped me dress, ordered
Netflix, paid the bills, assembled
jigsaw puzzles with me.

Now, I sit alone, staring
at the silver urn on the hearth.
All that's left of fifty-four
years of companionship.

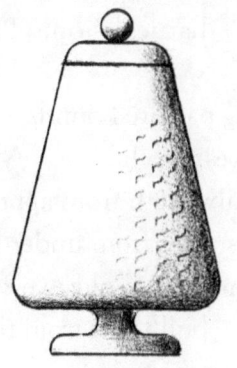

Tribute to Father's Hands

(Daniel Wiens 1893-1984)

Gaunt, wrinkled hands, diary of earlier days; every callous, every
scar a segment of history.

Diggers of
>> potatoes for the cellar
>>> cisterns for drinking water
>>>> fishing worms for eager boys
>>>>> post holes for pasture fence
>>>>>> graves for beloved friends

Swingers of
>> Model T crank on frozen mornings
>>> yellow hickory bat
>>>> ax against Osage orange for firewood
>>>>> giggling pigtailed daughter in arm-stretched
>>>>>> circles

Throwers of
>> plowed-up rocks onto flatbed wagon
>>> dirt stained baseball to budding Ruths
>>>> wheat bundles into gaping threshing machine
>>>>> fishing lines into the Cottonwood River
>>>>>> forked manure onto rented spreader
>>>>>>> harnesses onto Prince and Nell

Pullers of
>> barbed wire along pasture bounds
>>> half-born calves into life
>>>> wobbly baby teeth from apprehensive mouths
>>>>> rattlesnakes from under limestone rocks
>>>>>> throttle on old Avery steam engine
>>>>>>> bullheads from the farm pond

Holders of
second-hand fiddle
fuzzy yellow chicks
crying son with cut finger
sweat-preserved horses' reins
grieving friends
Mother's arthritic hands, now cold
the family Bible, faded and worn

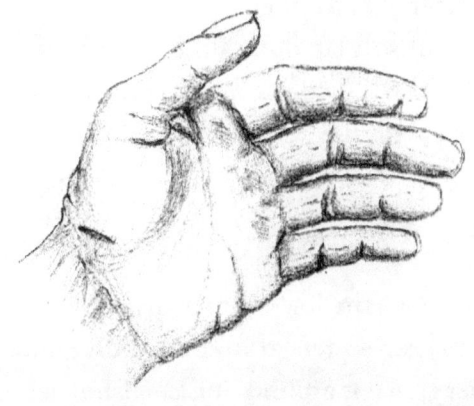

How Do I Remember You, Mother?

(Katherine Ediger Wiens -1901-1975)

How do I remember you, Mother?
>Arthritis robbed you of your middle years after I
>was born. Yet you toiled deliberately and faithfully,
>your pleasant smile masking your pain.

How do I remember you, Mother?
>I remember your soft lap during the German sermons
>before World War II (which I never understood).
>You cooled me with the "Good Shepherd" fans, on tepid
>Sunday eves.

How do I remember you, Mother?
>You and Pop spoke the low-country dialect.
>You used it to keep secrets, thinking I didn't understand,
>but you never spoke it around our English neighbors.

How do I remember you, Mother?
>The summer garden was your domain.
>You lumbered to the task with measured steps.
>I covered the seeds you planted with my little hands.

Peas, beans, carrots, corn, cucumbers, melons:
>drops of sweat watered the furrows and mingled
>with tomato juice over the wood-burning range as you
>prepared food for those days when the ground would be
>barren and white.

How do I remember you, Mother?
    Your kitchen contributed generously~
    ethnic zwieback, maple rolls for the threshing crew;
    Joe said, "Kate, those are the best damn maple rolls I ever et!"

How do I remember you, Mother?
    You taught me to mind the chickens:
    gather eggs, carry water, butcher the spring chickens:
    a simple chop with the corn knife,

a convulsing, blood-spurting form, more alive in dying than in life.
    Into scalding water to loosen the feathers,
    just in time for the hay-stackers' lunch,
    and, if a hen, later for noodle-making from undelivered eggs.

How do I remember you, Mother?
    You rendered the lard and cooked spare ribs in the black
    caldron.
    You cleaned the intestines for sausage casings
    and stuffed them with ground pork and liverwurst.

How do I remember you, Mother?
    You surprised us all with a duet at the community program.
    Silent Night, Pop on the fiddle, you on a Jews-harp.
    A standing ovation! (I never heard you practice.)

How do I remember you, Mother?
    You fixed food for grieving friends,
    tatted beautiful doilies for the bureau,
    and sewed clothes for little people somewhere;

How do I remember you, Mother?
    on your swollen knees, head bowed,
    Bible in hand
    praying for us all.

What did you teach me, Mother?
    With your sense of wonder, you taught me curiosity.
    With your disease, you taught me perseverance.
    With your humor, you taught me not to take myself too
    seriously.

With your example, you taught me
    that God loves all people, no exceptions.

The Old Barn

Part I - 1940

Weather-beaten siding boards silver as my father's hair.
Red-brown cancers festering on the galvanized roof.
Like generations before us, we lifted the rusting latch and
swung open the cow barn door; the dirt floor
hard packed by ten thousand hooves;

wooden stanchions polished amber by cow skin oil.
Cats sat upright here trapping warm,
airborne milk in gaping mouths.
Bro and I perched on our three-legged stools,
capped heads buried in bovine flanks, singing duets.

The bent roller track no longer supported the
wide, sliding door in the middle section
where the tractor and harvester hibernated.
An almost-concentric basketball hoop above the
bent track recalls winning baskets

by a half-empty basketball in the dead of winter.
To the left, an oats bin--the first of three.
A subculture of rats and mice claimed
the shallow crawl space beneath the grain bins.
It was here that I, a lad of 12,

hid a pack of Bull Durham tobacco
to sneak a smoke--a rite of manhood passage.
But the pack disappeared, and a generation
of rats annihilated by cancer.
Was it divine intervention?

Prince and Nell, the last titans to occupy
the horse stalls in the west section
rendered obsolete by petroleum and steel,
became dog food, fertilizer, and glue.
An unfitting end for such a marvelous pair,

pulling beyond their potential; mischievous,
lifting newborn calves by their ears.
So reliable, dependable, those grass-burners.
When they aroused a hive of bumble bees,
dump rakes were not made for that kind of speed!

Three sets of horse stalls converted to calf pens
where young offspring, newly orphaned
gained nourishment through a rubber nipple,
showed youth rebellion, bucking the bucket
and showering my clothes with splashed milk.

A ladder in a dark hallway
led to a hayloft above the calf pens.
Sweet alfalfa aroma descended
as I climbed the rungs to the loft.
Once the repository of forked hay,

now filled with rectangular bales
that made their entry via electric motor.
The haying crew now obsolete. For
children, the loft promised caves and tunnels.
A single light bulb blocked by bales

produced an eerie darkness
with frightening surprises—a
screaming tom cat, a visiting raccoon
surprised in a tunnel. A homeless vagrant
more imagined than real.

Part II – 1970

The faint smell of cows' flanks still
lingers in the abandoned barn.
The hayloft empty save for scattered hay
fragments. The basketball hoop on the ground
half covered by creeping buffalo grass.

The Allis Chalmers tractor and combine
relegated to the salvage yard.
The nipple on the calf bucket brittle and cracked.
Straw on the earthen floor once yellow,
now gray with wind-blown dust.

Rusting cancers on the metal roof
now metastasized, exposing blue sky.
Limestone foundation splintered and crumbling.

Part III – 2000

A half century now passed. The old barn—flat:
crinkled sheet metal, splintered wood, weeds.
Fences gone, corral sprouting winter wheat.
The windmill and stock tank, machine shed
and privy, gone--a mirage of memory now.

Only the fluent mockingbird atop the
deserted house can provide the
oral history of how it all happened.

Missing Events

Your Grand Opening came and went. I didn't.
Missed three events last week:
flute recital, your grand opening, a funeral,
only an old cousin, he probably didn't notice.

Is this a subconscious need~
to miss scheduled events?
But I meet doctors' appointments;
they require my presence, concerts don't.

Now retired, I expected to attend
all the concerts, not just my grandson's,
all the grand openings, not just the ones
with free food and entertainment.

By the time I reach 80,
you'll have to pry me off the couch
and push me out the door
in time for my own funeral.

My Funeral Prayer

Too late for my soul!
Either I'm in or out, can't change it now.
(Or do ins and outs not exist in the after-death?)
But I'll want a prayer for the soul of the world,
a world that has lost its way of compassion
and love, tolerance and justice for all human kind,
and respect and care for the earth.

If the pastor asks my favorite scripture:
paraphrase Apostle Paul:
"I saw through a glass darkly,
for my journey has been marked
by religious astigmatism,
but with a desire to comprehend
the unknowable."

31st and Gillham

The siren screams past the Empire Room
and the Velvet Dog, slows for 31st and Gillham,
turns right past the House of Flowers.
What beckons you out on this frigid night?

A flaming crash on 71,
victim of Kansas City road rage?
A carful of bottle-empty teenagers
racing a semi to the intersection?
A father with a van packed, vacation bound,
intent on reaching Columbia before midnight;
victim of a sleepless night and a sudden lamp post?

A drug deal gone sour?
A marriage that should never have happened?
Or for the man whose joy in life has expired,
whose inward focus has shut out the beauty of living?
Or is it for the silver-haired grandmother
who ate her last chocolate?

Your siren wails for us all.

Childhood Memories

The Boat[2]

Hansen's pond without a boat
was hardly fit for kids,
Until we spied Ol' Ernie's boat
a rottin' on some skids.

Aha! We'll fix 'er up, we thought,
and begged Ol' Ernie blind.
He grinned and winked and said, "One buck!"
as we explored our find.

The bill of sale was drawn at once
to make the promise stick.
"John Henry" he scrawled across the page;
Harry and I signed quick.

It was a tank, it weighed a ton,
that twelve foot wooden boat.
We'd need a hoist and pickup truck;
Three miles before she'd float.

But beg we wouldn't and thought the harder
'till we devised a plan.
We walked three miles to Hansen's house
on scorching roadside sand.

Two wagon wheels with axle stout
began the long road back.
Streams of sweat soon soaked our shorts;
we slowly rolled the hack.

2   First version published in A. Emerson Wiens, Mad Bulls, Skinny Dipping, and God, 2012, pp.146-147

Ol' Ernie helped us balance the boat
across the axle wide,
Got us started - me at the bow
and Harry at the side.

Six miles beneath the Kansas sun
began to take their toll.
We pushed and groaned and staggered on,
dodging every hole.

We stopped to drink and rest a bit
beneath the spreading hedge.
The sun was sinking in the west
when we reached the river's edge.

We fell exhausted to the ground.
Then, not thinking it was rude,
Both stood, peeled off our dirt-caked clothes,
went swimming in the nude.

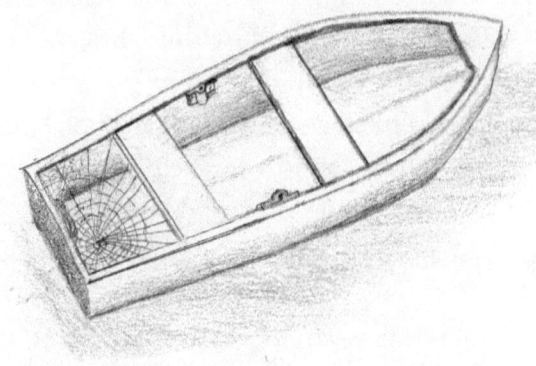

The Inebriated Cat

Young Harold was a curious boy
who never missed a chance
to learn some great and wondrous truth
but at his cat's expense.

A drunken cat he wished to see,
but cats are wiser than man,
reject the spirits, given a choice,
a most intelligent clan!

One day he took his favorite cat
(his name was Fritz the Third)
and lashed him to a red oak plank.
His howling could be heard

For miles around that Kansas farm
No rescue was in sight.
His sinews strained against the twine;
his eyes were wide with fright.

Harold filled a syringe with alcohol,
then found a tiny vein;
forced the lethal fluid in,
stepped back to watch the pain.

Old Fritz began to jerk and twitch,
and Harold released the bond.
Fritz in drunken stupor staggered
senseless toward the pond.

Then Papa came upon the scene.
"A rabid cat!" he thought;
dispatched the cat with a single blow.
Harold was distraught.

The Chamber Pot

White enameled nighttime guest,
Unsung hero of bathroomless;
Receives deposits quite unblest
So folks at night can get their rest.

Dog Biscuits

She loves dog biscuits,
my beautiful German Shepherd.
And she's astonishingly literate;
When I ask, "Dog biscuit?"

She goes wild,
leading the way to the
box on the shelf
beyond her reach.

"Not so fast," I tease,
grabbing her muzzle
tweaking her ears,
pulling her tail.

It's a game we play.
She thinks it's harassment.

My Room

"Your room is an absolute mess!"
My mother announced in distress.
"Your toys and your clothes are left piled
all over the floor, and I'm riled!
Your new shoes are muddy and torn.
What's that on the top? It looks foreign.
Is that a green apple, all wrinkled and brown?
Or yesterday's wheat toast?" she points with a frown.
"There's a ball glove and bat and catcher's mask, too;
dead butterflies, rabbit feet, puzzles and glue;
New baseball cards, marbles, dried fishing worms, books
of jungle adventures, smart spies and dumb crooks!
Something strange in that pile will be born
if it's not cleaned up before morn!"

Nature and Others

Flint Hills Brook

An eager child, the brook,
leaps from pool to pool
driven by an invisible force;
a carnival mirror, undulating,
tumbling over rocks rounded
by centuries of churning water.

Limestone and flint divert
the raucous flow into minute Niagaras.
Bubbles burst to the surface,
float quietly past the shelter
of a rock only to be captured
again by the boiling current.

In the eddies, rocks replaced
by sand and gravel.
The speeding current tugs at the
stubborn water along the bank
that has found its peace
in placid pools.

The water artist brushes
flint rocks charcoal black,
contrasting limestone cream,
with hints of red-orange oxide.
Last fall's leaves shine deep brown
in the eddies, awaiting decay.

Shimmering flashes of sunlight,
demonstrate the partnership between
sun and water, a partnership begun
when earth moisture becomes spirit
rising toward the sun, returning
as droplets and flakes to renew and refresh.

The flint hills brook,
chasing, pouncing, rolling~
the sun and the stream,
flashing, splashing,
shimmering, reflecting, dancing.

List Poem: Things that Change Color with Age

Fresh bread and hair of red;
white socks and limestone rocks;
teacher's notes and silver broach;
yellow cheese and maple leaves;
rainbow bright and evening light;
downy chicks and fender nicks;
kitten's eyes and denim dyes;
polished brass and bluestem grass;
spotted fawns and summer lawns.

BLUESTEM[1]

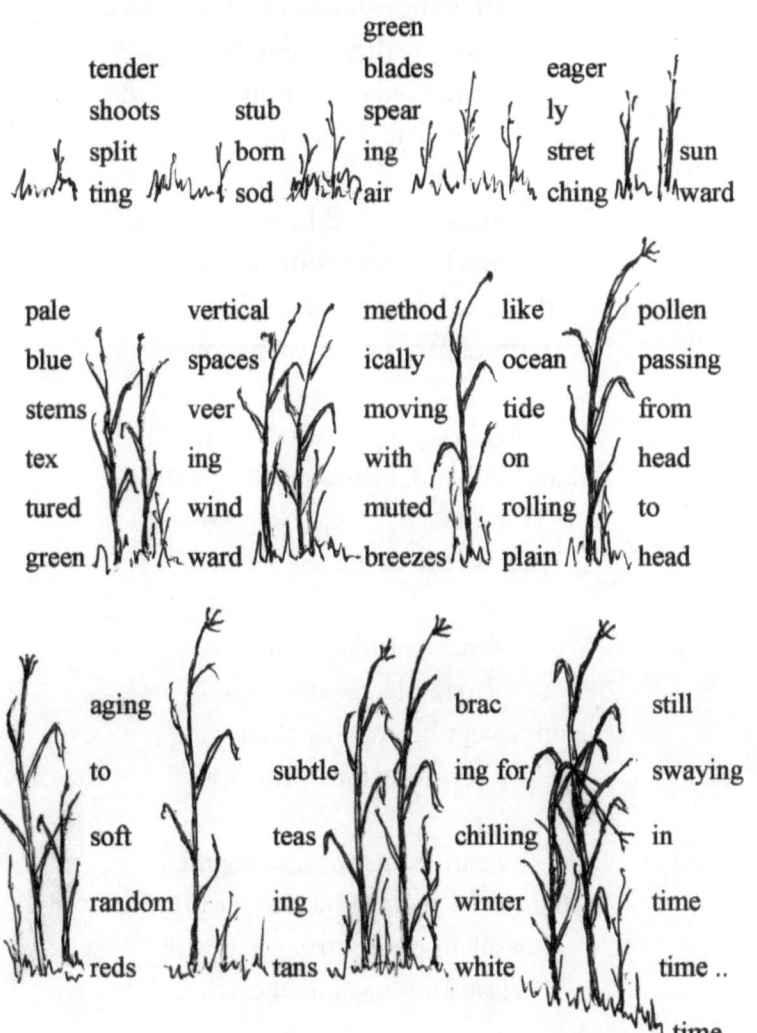

green
tender   blades   eager
shoots   stub   spear   ly
split   born   ing   stret   sun
ting   sod   air   ching   ward

pale   vertical   method   like   pollen
blue   spaces   ically   ocean   passing
stems   veer   moving   tide   from
tex   ing   with   on   head
tured   wind   muted   rolling   to
green   ward   breezes   plain   head

aging   brac   still
to   subtle   ing for   swaying
soft   teas   chilling   in
random   ing   winter   time
reds   tans   white   time ..
                          time ...

1

First published in the Ninth Annual Issue of *Oberon Poetry Magazine*, 2011, p. 32. Used by permission.

Morning Walk

The mottled orange and black cat follows us
down the drive, hesitates,
slips under the cedars that line the road.
She will await our return.

Wood chips, bleached by sun and rain
crunch beneath our shoes.
Rustling leaves above recite tales
of times past, events yet to come.

My bride of 57 years and I,
hand in hand, begin our daily walk.
"On the left," a bicycle passes.
Yet we are in our own world.

A dozen turkey vultures
circle silently above us
imperceptibly moving their wings,
sniffing for death.

The path turns west, along the
drought-stricken creek no longer flowing.
Now silent pools dirty green with
algae and suspended earth

belie the community below the surface.
Two carp as long as my forearm, noisily
work the far bank, searching for morsels,
desired by no other creatures.

The olive-brown snout of a soft-shelled turtle
protrudes through the glass surface;
examines the environment, sinks quietly,
in search of flesh, decaying or alive.

Water spiders stride across the pool
on stilted legs while glossy black
water bugs career about in patterns
that only they understand or maybe not.

A great blue heron, knee deep, motionless,
eyes fixed on life below the surface,
awaiting movement of the unwary
for her breakfast.

Suddenly the surface ripples;
A hundred tiny catfish
squiggling behind their mother.
She sees our movement, drops from sight

magnetically drawing her young
down with her. I wonder~ how is
the under-water community organized?
Or is organization a human construct?

Much I don't know about the under-water.
We reach the railroad trestle
now dammed by floating brush.
An American egret atop the railroad tracks~

brilliant white against sky blue~follows our
every move. We retrace our steps.
The mottled feline, emerging from the cedars,
greets us at the drive.

Kansas Wind

Pink mimosa fronds wave gently.
Ripples stretch across the pond propelled by the
Kansas breeze. Prairie grasses bow and rise in
adulation, homage to the wind god.

Gentle was not your name in the 30's.
Fury was your character.
Noon hour became midnight.
Street lights helpless in your presence.

Topsoil rolled relentlessly over
the plains~the black blizzard~
burying everything in its path,
bringing dust pneumonia to the crib.

What transgression brought such fate?
White man destroying Red Man's habitat?
Man defiling nature's balance?
How do we seek forgiveness?

Catfishing

Stretched out on a sand bar; sun now gone.
Levis wretched from stink bait and river slime.
Sweat trickles on our bare chests now dry.

Mostly we rest on our elbows, listening to the night.
Welcoming the emerging stars; suspicioning
movement in the shadows on the far bank,

listening apprehensively
to the unexplained rustle in the
head-high itch-weed behind us.

Thin nylon line between thumb
and forefinger,
we wait for catfish.

Allerton Park

Sculptured hedges, espalier pears,
red-orange-yellow day-lilies,
blue-glazed Fu dogs; concrete, oriental carp
with gaping throats and split tails.
Grinning dwarf pipers lining the walk,
bluegills in the pond snatching
careless grasshoppers.
The same as they did 40 years ago.
Yet not. Day-lilies for a season;
New generations of bluegills;
hedges uprooted, replaced.

You were a boy then.
Curious; boundless, explosive energy;
Chasing squirrels, butterflies, time.
Gently smelling the roses, noisily
cracking acorns as you bounded
down the forest path,
breathlessly watching deer grazing~
fleeting moments. Riding the concrete centaur
through dark forests, across strange
valleys into unforeseen battles.
So it was then when we passed this way.
It will never be the same.

Amtrak Across Northern Montana

(Heading East)

Azure blue lakes reflect the morning sky.
The Empire Builder swallowed by pines
straight as flagpoles, touching the clouds.
Trout streams and rivers tumble past seeking the Missouri.
Glaciers present but unseen, now speed behind us.
Jolt, sway, bump, squeak.

Dry land ranches reach the horizon;
rolling hills, treeless landscape,
white horses, black angus in contrast.
A lonely five-point on the periphery.
Jolt, sway, bump, squeak.

No longer white-cottaged farms
dwarfed by towering green.
Mammoth mechanical contraptions circle
thousand-acre fields of yellow wheat.
Jolt, sway, bump, squeak.

Forest-green alfalfa sucking water
from underground lakes. A metallic
hen devours rows of cut hay, laying giant
spools wrapped in marigold netting.

A frame house, once white, miniaturized by
Montana expanse, stands alone surrounded
by silent vehicles, dead ants around the ant hill,
now prisoners of the yard.

Morning Solitude

I hear the distant bobwhites calling
before I stretch out of bed.
The natural world, fully alive,
beckons me to join.

The mocking bird, perched on the peak
of the roof, ushers in the morning
with its song, mocking only himself.
The air, crisp and inviting,

meets me at the open door.
The cobblestone path begs me
follow down the hill to the
flowing brook that pays

no attention to my presence.
Footprints pressed into
the yellow clay bank~
evidence of nighttime shoppers

surveying the stream menu
while the hound slept.
The overhead croak of the night heron
winging its way upstream,

demonstrating that all creatures
have their own meal schedule.
A bullfrog with broad green back,
sits motionlessly except for

its pulsating cream-colored throat,
resting from half a night of
conversation, daring a careless fly
to land on the twig before him.

Autumn

Leaving the work list behind me,
I step out on the deck.
The air, crisp and invigorating.
The magic of the season inundates
the environment. The wand of autumn
has passed over my world.

Overnight, the sugar maple green
is brushed with a palette of intense
yellow-reds, and the delicate leaves
of the amur maple are a blazing crimson.
The cottonwoods that surround the pond
shimmer gold in the morning sun.

A sense of serenity and peace permeates
my being. I am one with the beauty that
surrounds me. Yet, my conservative religion
causes me to question whether I
deserve such joy; but this is God's world,
not a creation of acrylic and steel.

My life, however inspired by the season,
will go on. The job list awaits,
the brilliance of autumn will fade;
the trees will release their leaves,
the copper tones of the tall bluestem
will be a diminished tan by winter white.

Writer's Block

I seek to write
of God above and mother's love,
of grandma's tears and childhood fears.

I seek to write
of morning dew and skies of blue;
of fields of grass and sunsets past.

I seek to write
of redneck hate and alligator bait;
assassin plots and kidnapped tots.

I seek to write
of sewage swills and offshore spills;
altar boy crimes and priestly lies.

I seek to write,
of family ties to foreign spies;
hot romances and second chances,

but no words come.